Martin Luther King, Jr.
THE FIGHT FOR FREEDOM

ISBN 0-439-66830-1

Text copyright © 2004 by Joanne Mattern
Illustrations copyright © 2004 by Robert F. Goetzl

All rights reserved. Published by Scholastic Inc.

SCHOLASTIC and associated logos are trademarks and/or
registered trademarks of Scholastic Inc.

12 11 10 9 8 7 6 5 4   5 6 7 8 9/0

Printed in the U.S.A.

First Printing, October 2004

Martin Luther King, Jr.
THE FIGHT FOR FREEDOM

SCHOLASTIC INC.

New York   Toronto   London   Auckland   Sydney
Mexico City   New Delhi   Hong Kong   Buenos Aires

TABLE OF CONTENTS

CHAPTER 1:
A Child's Dream

Little Yolanda King was excited. The six-year-old girl had seen a television commercial for an amusement park in Atlanta, Georgia, called Funtown. It looked like a wonderful place. "Please, Daddy, can we go?" she begged.

Yolanda's father, Martin Luther King, Jr., shook his head sadly. "No, sweetheart, we can't go to Funtown," he told her.

"Why not?" the little girl asked.

"Because Funtown is only open to white people," Martin said. "Black people like us aren't allowed to go there."

Yolanda began to cry. "That's not fair," she said.

"No, it isn't fair," Martin told her. He cried, too. "There are a lot of places where black people can't go. Daddy and lots of other people are

working to change that." Martin gave Yolanda a big hug. "Meanwhile, remember, you are as good as anybody else. Everyone is important, no matter what the color of their skin."

Martin had faced prejudice and discrimination all his life. And all his life, he worked to change things so that black people and white people would be treated equally.

CHAPTER 2:
Little M.L.

Martin Luther King, Jr., was born in Atlanta, on January 15, 1929. His father was a minister named Martin Luther King, Sr. He was the pastor of the Ebenezer Baptist Church. Martin's mother, Alberta King, played the organ at Ebenezer. Church was always an important part of Martin's life. His father was an excellent speaker. Martin loved sitting in church, listening to his father's powerful words.

The King family also included Martin's brother, Alfred Daniel; his sister, Christine; his grandparents; and several aunts and uncles. The King home was crowded, but it was filled with love and happiness.

When Martin was growing up, everyone called him "M.L." M.L. was a tough kid. Once, his brother accidentally hit him in the head with a baseball bat during a game. M.L. fell down. But then he jumped right back up and kept playing.

M.L.'s father was strict but fair. He taught M.L. to work hard. He also made sure M.L. and his brother and sister were proud of who they were. The King family respected themselves, even in tough times.

It was hard for a black family in Atlanta to feel pride and self-respect. In those days, the southern part of the United States was segregated. Laws kept black people and white people apart. Black people had their own public bathrooms, water fountains, and swimming pools. They could not sit in certain seats on buses or trains. Blacks and whites could not go to the same schools. If a black customer wanted to buy something in a store, he or she had to wait until all the white customers were waited on first.

When M.L. was a little boy, he was good friends with two white boys. The boys had a lot of fun playing together. Then one day, when M.L. went to the boys' house, their mother would

not let him in. "You can't play with my sons anymore," she said. "We're white and you're colored."

M.L. didn't understand why the color of his skin made him different from other people. He went home, crying. M.L.'s mother told him that blacks had once been slaves. Even though slavery was outlawed in 1863, many white people still felt blacks were not as good as they were. M.L.'s mother told him that was not true. "You're as good as anyone else," she said.

Like other black children, M.L. went to a segregated school. He was very smart and skipped

several grades. Martin started college when he was only 15 years old. By then, people were calling him Martin instead of M.L. Everyone knew he had a bright future ahead of him.

CHAPTER 3:
Looking for Answers

Martin went to Morehouse College in Atlanta. Everyone thought Martin would be a minister like his father. But Martin wanted to be a doctor

or a lawyer. He wanted to help people and change unfair laws.

When he was in college, Martin asked many questions. His teachers let him explore many different subjects.

By the time he was 17, Martin saw that ministers could be powerful people who could change society. Martin told his family, "I want to be a minister, just like Daddy."

To be a minister, Martin had to go to a special school called a seminary. Martin went to Crozier

Theological Seminary in Chester, Pennsylvania.
The schools in Pennsylvania were not segregated
like the schools in the South. Martin had white
teachers. He made white friends. And he studied
hard every day. The more he learned, the more
questions he had. "How can one person change
the world?" Martin asked. "How can I love people
who hurt me?"

Then Martin read about a man named Mahatma
Gandhi. Gandhi lived in India. India was ruled

by Great Britain, and the Indian people faced many unfair laws, just like black people in the United States. Gandhi worked hard to change those laws. Some people used violence to try to change things. But Gandhi believed that peaceful protests worked better. He did not hate people, no matter what they did to him. In time, India won its independence from Great Britain.

Martin understood what Gandhi was trying to say. He saw that he could love people but still hate the things they did. Martin decided that he would use peaceful ways to change segregation and other unfair conditions in the United States.

CHAPTER 4:
Martin Meets Coretta

Martin graduated from Crozier Theological Seminary in 1951. His family wanted him to come back to Atlanta and be the assistant pastor of Ebenezer Baptist Church. But Martin had other plans. He wanted to learn more. In September, Martin started school at Boston University in Boston, Massachusetts. He studied theology. And he kept asking questions.

As always, Martin did very well in school. But he made time for fun, too. He went out to eat with his friends. He danced at clubs and went to concerts all over Boston.

One day, Martin's friend told him about a smart, pretty girl named Coretta Scott. Coretta was studying music at another school in Boston. As soon as Martin met Coretta, he fell in love with her. He even asked Coretta to marry him on

their first date! But Coretta was not so sure she wanted to marry Martin. She thought he was a show-off who talked too much. She also didn't want to be a minister's wife. She wanted to be a concert singer.

In time, however, Coretta fell in love with Martin. On June 18, 1953, Martin's father married Coretta and Martin at Coretta's home in Marion, Alabama. Then the young couple returned to Boston to finish school.

Many people thought Martin should become a teacher when he finished school. But Martin wanted to be the pastor of a church. Coretta agreed but hoped he would take a job in a northern church. Life was much easier for blacks in the North, and she could continue her singing career there. Things didn't work out that way, however.

Martin received an offer to become the pastor of the Dexter Avenue Baptist Church in Montgomery, Alabama.

Coretta and Martin's family did not want him to take the job. Montgomery was even more segregated than Atlanta. Coretta had grown up in Alabama, and she knew how difficult life there could be for black people. But Martin felt drawn back to the South. "We can't make things better for Southern black people if we aren't living down there with them," he told Coretta. She agreed. In 1954, Martin and Coretta moved to Montgomery. The move would change their lives forever.

CHAPTER 5:
The Bus Boycott

Big things were about to happen in Montgomery. Like other Southern cities, the buses in Montgomery were segregated. White people sat in the front of the bus, and black people sat in the back. If all the seats were taken, black passengers had to give up their seats to white passengers.

On December 1, 1955, a woman named Rosa Parks got on a crowded bus. She was on her way home from her job at a department store. Rosa found a seat in the back. Then more white passengers got on. The driver stopped the bus and asked Rosa to give up her seat.

Rosa was tired of giving up her rights. "No, I will not get up. I paid for this seat and I have the same right to sit here as anyone else," she said.

"You don't have any rights," the bus driver told her. "If you don't give up your seat, I'll have you arrested." "You may do that," Rosa said. The driver called the police and Rosa Parks was arrested. As soon as Martin and other black leaders in Montgomery heard what had happened, they rushed into action. Martin met with members of the National Association for the Advancement of Colored People, or NAACP. The NAACP decided to take Rosa's case all the way to the U.S. Supreme Court. They wanted to prove that the bus segregation law in Montgomery was illegal.

Meanwhile, Martin and other ministers met with black leaders. They decided to boycott the buses on Monday, December 5. Leaflets were quickly printed and handed out to the black community. That Sunday, Martin told his congregation not to ride the buses the next day. Although his words were strong and sure, Martin was nervous. Would people really boycott the buses and walk?

The answer was yes! On Monday, only eight black people rode Montgomery's buses. The others walked, got rides from friends, or took cabs to get to work and school. Some people even rode mules! Martin and the other leaders were delighted. They decided to continue the boycott until the bus company treated blacks and whites equally.

That night, 26-year-old Martin spoke to a packed church. He told everyone that the boycott would be a powerful protest against unfair laws. But there would not be any violence. "Love must be our regulating ideal," he said. It was a lesson he never forgot.

CHAPTER 6:
Danger!

Martin and his followers would not use violence, but many white people in Montgomery would. They threatened to hurt black people. The police arrested people waiting for rides and ticketed drivers who picked up black passengers. Then, on January

30, 1956, someone bombed Martin's house. Martin wasn't home, but Coretta and their three-month-old daughter, Yolanda, barely escaped from the burning house.

When Martin got home, he found an angry crowd of blacks waiting for him. They wanted to fight the people who had done this terrible thing. But Martin told them no.

"Remember, if I'm stopped, this movement will not stop," he said. Martin was scared for himself and his family. But he knew he could not stop his fight for justice.

The Montgomery bus boycott lasted for eleven months. Finally, in November 1956, the Supreme Court made its decision. The highest court in the United States said that segregated buses were illegal. Martin and his followers had won! Their nonviolent protest had changed an unfair law.

Martin's victory in Montgomery made him famous all over America. Black leaders in other cities followed his nonviolent example to change laws in their communities. When a group of Southern black ministers formed a group called the Southern Christian Leadership Conference (SCLC), they elected Martin as their president. Martin was an important young man now!

CHAPTER 7:
Family and Fame

On May 17, 1957, Martin spoke to more than 20,000 people at the civil-rights rally in front of the Lincoln Memorial in Washington, D.C. Martin's words electrified the crowd. Newspapers all over the world reported what he said. From then on, Martin was asked to speak at events all over the country.

Martin's personal life was busy, too. After Yolanda was born in 1955, he and Coretta had three more children: Martin Luther King III, Dexter, and Bernice. In 1959, Martin and his family moved back to Atlanta. Martin worked with his father at Ebenezer Baptist Church.

He wrote several books. And he led many protest marches to fight against inequality.

Sometimes Coretta traveled with Martin. But usually she stayed at home with the children. It was a difficult and lonely life for her. However, she was proud of Martin's work and knew he was making a difference in the world.

Martin's work made many people angry. He was arrested more than two hundred times. In April 1963, Martin went to Birmingham, Alabama. He

and his brother led more than fifteen hundred people in a civil-rights march. Martin was arrested and sent to jail. While he was there, he wrote a document called "A Letter from a Birmingham Jail." In it, Martin said

34

that there were two kinds of laws. Some laws were just. Others were unjust. Martin stated that people should obey just laws but that they had "a legal and moral responsibility to disobey unjust laws." Martin's "Letter" became one of the most famous protest documents in history.

CHAPTER 8:
"I Have a Dream"

On August 28, 1963, Martin appeared at the largest civil-rights demonstration in United States history. More than 250,000 people gathered between the Washington Monument and the Lincoln Memorial in Washington, D.C. Millions more watched on television. The event was called the March on Washington, and many important black leaders were there.

Many people spoke to the huge crowd. Some had lost family members to racial violence. Others were important black leaders, such as A. Philip Randolph, founder of a union representing black workers on trains. Rosa Parks was there. Famous singers Marian Anderson and Mahalia Jackson led the crowd in song.

Martin's turn to speak came at the end of the

program. He had written a speech, but when he stood in front of the crowd, he decided not to read it. Instead, he spoke what he was feeling in his heart, making up the words as he went along.

"I have a dream my four little children will one day live in a nation where they will not be

judged by the color of their skin but by the content of their character," he told the crowd. He asked everyone to join him in the fight for freedom. "Let freedom ring," Martin said.

"When we allow freedom to ring, when we let it ring from every village and every hamlet, from every state and every city, we will be able to speed up that day when *all* of God's children— black men and white men, Jews and Gentiles, Protestants and Catholics—will be able to join hands and sing in the words of the old Negro spiritual, 'Free at last, free at last, thank God Almighty, we are free at last.'"

The crowd was deeply affected by Martin's words. They cheered Martin's powerful message. Many people cried. It was a day none of them would ever forget.

CHAPTER 9:
The Promised Land

Martin was proud of how his words had moved the crowd in Washington. He knew his work was changing unfair laws in a peaceful way. Sometimes these changes touched his family. A few days before Christmas 1963, Martin was able to take his daughter Yolanda to Funtown. The amusement park was finally open to all.

In 1964, Martin won the Nobel Peace Prize. Martin and his whole family traveled to Norway to receive this tremendous honor. Martin donated the prize money to

several civil-rights organizations. Then he jumped right back into his work.

Martin continued to work hard for the next four years. He spent many nights away from his family. He faced violence and anger from people who did not agree with him. Still, he kept working. He knew that the only way to achieve his dream was to give everything he had to make it come true.

Martin knew he had many enemies. He worried that someone would try to kill him. A man had killed Martin's hero, Mahatma Gandhi, because he did not agree with Gandhi's ideas. Martin's speeches gave hints that he would not see his dream fulfilled. "I've seen the Promised Land," he said in his last public speech. "I may not get there with you. But I want you to know that we as a people will get to the Promised Land."

In April 1968, Martin was in Memphis, Tennessee, to lead another march. This time, he was working with poor black sanitation employees who were going on strike for better pay and working conditions. About 5:30 P.M. on April 4, Martin

was getting ready to go out to dinner with his friends. He stepped out onto the balcony of his hotel room. Suddenly, a gunshot rang out. Martin fell to the floor. He died in a Memphis hospital an hour and a half later. Martin was 39 years old.

On April 8, Coretta led the march that Martin had planned to lead. Then she brought her husband's body back to Atlanta, where he was buried on April 9. One hundred thousand people surrounded Ebenezer Baptist Church for the service. All over the country, blacks and whites wept as if they had lost a dear friend.

Two months later, a white man named James Earl Ray was arrested for Martin's murder. He was found guilty and spent the rest of his life in prison.

CHAPTER 10:
Martin Lives On

Martin Luther King, Jr., changed many things in his short life. His actions changed laws and made conditions better for black people and poor people all over the country. He also showed people that peaceful actions could overpower violence and hatred. Martin's life became a shining example of the power of love.

Martin's ideas live on today. Coretta helped create the Martin Luther King, Jr., Center for Nonviolent Social Change in Atlanta. The King Center includes many activities for children and their families to learn about nonviolence. The King Center also sponsors programs to educate the public about nonviolence and social change.

Cities and towns all over America honored
Martin. They named schools, parks, and memorials
after him. A postage stamp was issued in his

honor. Finally, in 1983, President Ronald Reagan signed a law making Martin's birthday a national holiday. On the third Monday of each January, we celebrate Martin Luther King, Jr., Day. It is a time to reflect on Martin's life and work. Communities celebrate the day with musical performances and speeches. People give their time to others on that day by working on projects to improve their communities. It is the perfect way to honor a man who dedicated his life to helping others be treated fairly.